Y0-EFZ-084

WITHDRAWN

My World of ANIMALS™

NATASHYA WILSON

HUNTINGTON CITY-TOWNSHIP
PUBLIC LIBRARY
200 W. Market Street
Huntington IN 46750

The Rosen Publishing Group's
PowerKids Press™
New York

1

For Dad, a.k.a. Père, happy birthday!

Published in 2004 by The Rosen Publishing Group, Inc.
29 East 21st Street, New York, NY 10010

Copyright © 2004 by The Rosen Publishing Group, Inc.

All rights reserved. No part of this book may be reproduced in any form without permission in writing from the publisher, except by a reviewer.

First Edition

Book Design: Mike Donnellan
Illustration by Mike Donnellan

Photo Credits: Cover, pp. 11, 13, 19, 22 © CORBIS; pp. 5, 7, 9, 15 © Digital Vision Ltd.; p. 17 © AP/Wide World Photos; p. 21 © Scott Wm. Hanrahan/International Stock.

Library of Congress Cataloging-in-Publication Data

Wilson, Natashya.
  Bears / Natashya Wilson.
      p. cm. – (My world of animals)
Includes index.
Summary: Provides an easy-to-read introduction to the life of bears and their habitat.
  ISBN 1-4042-2518-8 (library binding)
  1. Bears–Juvenile literature. [1. Bears.] I. Title. II. Series.
  QL737.C27 W56 2004
  599.78–dc21

                                                          2003007191

Manufactured in the United States of America

CONTENTS

This is a bear.

5

Bears roar. They have sharp teeth and big paws.

7

Some bears eat fish. They catch fish in rivers.

9

Some bears live in the mountains. This is a grizzly bear.

This is a polar bear. Polar bears live in very cold places. They walk on ice.

13

This is a panda bear.
Panda bears live in forests
and eat plants.

15

Some bears live in zoos
and have toys. This bear
has a ball.

17

Mother bears take care of their babies. A baby bear is called a cub.

19

This cub is watching its
mother swim. Bear cubs learn
from their mothers.

21

WORDS TO KNOW

cub

fish

mountains

teeth

Here are more books to read about bears:

Black Bears
Brown Bears
Famous Bears
Panda Bears
Polar Bears
by Diana Star Helmer
Rosen Publishing

Due to the changing nature of Internet links, PowerKids Press has developed an online list of Web sites related to the subject of this book. This site is updated regularly. Please use this link to access the list:

www.powerkidslinks.com/mwanim/bear/

HUNTINGTON CITY-TOWNSHIP
PUBLIC LIBRARY
200 W. Market Street
Huntington IN 46750

INDEX

Word Count: 102

Note to Parents, Teachers, and Librarians

PowerKids Readers are specially designed to help emergent and beginning readers build their skills in reading for information. Simple vocabulary and concepts are paired with real-life photographs or stunning, detailed images from the natural world. Readers will respond to written language by linking meaning with their own everyday experiences and observations. Sentences are short and simple, employing a basic vocabulary of sight words, as well as new words that describe objects or processes that take place in the natural world. Large type, clean design, and photographs corresponding directly to the text all help children to decipher meaning. Features such as a contents page, picture glossary, and index help children to get the most out of PowerKids Readers. They also introduce children to the basic elements of a book, which they will encounter in their future reading experiences. Lists of related books and Web sites encourage kids to explore other sources and to continue the process of learning.